# PUPPIES AND THEIR PARENTS

# PUPPIES AND THEIR PARENTS

## WISDOM AND INSPIRATION ABOUT ANY PARENT'S UNCONDITIONAL LOVE

SHAINA FISHMAN

Skyhorse Publishing

Skyhorse Publishing books may be purchased in bulk at special discounts for sales promotion, corporate gifts, fund-raising, or educational purposes. Special editions can also be created to specifications. For details, contact the Special Sales Department, Skyhorse Publishing, 307 West 36th Street, 11th Floor, New York, NY 10018 or info@skyhorsepublishing.com.

Skyhorse® and Skyhorse Publishing® are registered trademarks of Skyhorse Publishing, Inc.®, a Delaware corporation.

Visit our website at www.skyhorsepublishing.com.

10 9 8 7 6 5 4 3 2 1

Library of Congress Cataloging-in-Publication Data is available on file.

Cover design by Daniel Brount

Print ISBN: 978-1-5107-4944-3
Ebook ISBN: 978-1-5107-4946-7

Printed in China

**To Neve and Laine**

# INTRODUCTION

Relationships between dogs, just like those between humans, are dynamic and unique.

Growing up in a household that had at least two cats and two dogs at any given time, I had the privilege of watching relationships between pets unfold. As a young girl, I adopted a kitten and named him Yoni. He was the most energetic member of the household, and he forced the other cats and dogs to become his playmates. But as Yoni grew older, he lost interest in playing with the other animals. Even when two new dogs joined the family and wanted to play with him, he had no interest. Then, when Yoni was fifteen years old, Cosmo, a Papillon, became a part of the family. The playful kitten in Yoni was reignited. Cosmo would run circles around the ottoman as Yoni sat on it, pawing and teasing him. The renewed playfulness in that old cat was a delight to watch. Why was the relationship between Yoni and Cosmo different? Like in any relationship, human or animal, the reasons were unknown—they just clicked.

When I started this book, I wasn't sure how the images would come together. I had ideas, thoughts on how to approach each session, and poses for the pairs, and I planned as much as I could. However, I knew that the dogs' temperament and their relationships would dictate the photoshoot. I did not force anything to happen.

When dogs entered the studio they were flooded with stimuli: new people interested in playing with them, smells from past visitors, unusual-looking lighting equipment, and tons of space to claim as their own. I think of the most dogs believed the studio was some kind of strange dog park. Almost all the dogs were eager to play and explore the new and exciting space.

There was a certain amount of wrangling the dog duos, but the sessions were always based on the personality and relationship between the dogs. If the dogs wanted to run and jump, that was what I would capture. If they were docile and only interested in sitting, I would position and pose them. There was a broad spectrum of energy and pace between sessions. At one end, I was able to position and place every detail of the dog, from each paw to the way the ears flopped. The opposite end was the dogs that would not sit still, not even for a second.

The corgi puppies, Edison and Dallas, came into the studio with a burst of energy. They ran in circles and chased each other by sliding on the glossy floor and knocking into one another as their paths crossed. They were so caught up in their play that they didn't care about the camera and lights. I corralled their play session to capture their folly. Since they didn't pay attention to the space around them and just wanted to play with each other, the challenge in photographing these playmates was keeping them on the set.

Completely opposite the corgis were the pugs. Nena, the mom, did not care to incorporate Jack, the  puppy, into her moment in the spotlight. Jack wanted constant physical contact with Nena, and he would try to curl up next to her, but she paid no attention to him and went about her routine: sit, lie down, roll over, claim a treat, and repeat. As long as Jack didn't get in the way of her spotlight, she tolerated his presence. Once Nena was tired and full of treats, Jack was able to snuggle up to her for a nap.

The relationships between these dogs mirrors the dynamics we have in our family relationships. Within the images you can see love, annoyance, pride, and happiness. The relationships vary from loving and doting to playful and jovial. And most relatable to me as a mother of two young children, exhaustion.

# PUPPIES AND THEIR PARENTS

"YOU CAN LEARN MANY THINGS FROM CHILDREN.
HOW MUCH PATIENCE YOU HAVE, FOR INSTANCE."
—FRANKLIN P. JONES

"I ASK ONLY CHILD-FREE PALS FOR PARENTING ADVICE BECAUSE THEY'RE THE ONLY ONES SANE AND WELL-RESTED ENOUGH TO HAVE ANY REAL INSIGHT."
—GLENNON DOYLE MELTON

"WE NEVER KNOW THE LOVE OF A PARENT
TILL WE BECOME PARENTS OURSELVES."
—HENRY WARD BEECHER

"PARENTING IS LOVE, SURE, BUT IT'S AS MUCH ABOUT RECEIVING
LOVE AS IT IS GIVING IT. PARENTHOOD IS A KIND OF VANITY."

—RUMAAN ALAM

"WHEN MY KIDS BECOME UNRULY, I USE A NICE PLAYPEN.
WHEN THEY'RE FINISHED, I CLIMB OUT."
—ERMA BOMBECK

"90 PERCENT OF PARENTING IS JUST THINKING
ABOUT WHEN YOU CAN LIE DOWN AGAIN."
—ANONYMOUS

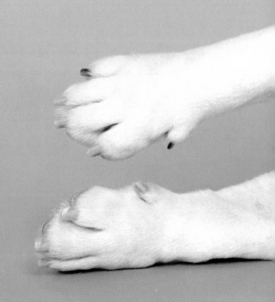

"MAKING A DECISION TO HAVE A CHILD . . .
IT'S MOMENTOUS. IT IS TO DECIDE FOREVER
TO HAVE YOUR HEART GO WALKING
OUTSIDE OF YOUR BODY."

—ELIZABETH STONE

"THE WAY WE TALK TO OUR CHILDREN
BECOMES THEIR INNER VOICE."
—PEGGY O'MARA

"THE QUICKEST WAY FOR A PARENT TO GET A CHILD'S ATTENTION IS TO SIT DOWN AND LOOK COMFORTABLE."

—LANE OLINGHOUSE

"THE BEST WAY TO MAKE
CHILDREN GOOD IS TO
MAKE THEM HAPPY."
—OSCAR WILDE

"HAVING ONE CHILD MAKES YOU A PARENT;
HAVING TWO, YOU ARE A REFEREE."

—DAVID FROST

"DON'T TRY TO MAKE CHILDREN GROW UP TO BE LIKE YOU,
OR THEY MAY DO IT."
—RUSSELL BAKER

"THERE IS NO SINGLE EFFORT MORE RADICAL
IN ITS POTENTIAL FOR SAVING THE WORLD
THAN A TRANSFORMATION OF THE WAY WE
RAISE OUR CHILDREN."

—MARIANNE WILLIAMSON

"TELL ME AND I FORGET, TEACH ME AND I MAY
REMEMBER, INVOLVE ME AND I LEARN."
—CHINESE PROVERB

"IT'S NOT OUR JOB TO TOUGHEN OUR CHILDREN UP TO FACE A CRUEL AND HEARTLESS WORLD. IT'S OUR JOB TO RAISE CHILDREN WHO WILL MAKE THE WORLD A LITTLE LESS CRUEL AND HEARTLESS."

—L. R. KNOST

"HAVING CHILDREN IS LIKE LIVING
IN A FRAT HOUSE. NOBODY SLEEPS,
EVERYTHING'S BROKEN, AND THERE'S
A LOT OF THROWING UP."

—RAY ROMANO

"HUGS CAN DO GREAT AMOUNTS OF GOOD—ESPECIALLY FOR CHILDREN."

—PRINCESS DIANA

"ALWAYS KISS YOUR CHILDREN GOODNIGHT,
EVEN IF THEY'RE ALREADY ASLEEP."

—H. JACKSON BROWN, JR.

"RAISING KIDS IS PART JOY AND
PART GUERILLA WARFARE."
—ED ASNER

"SAYING 'NO' TO YOUR CHILDREN
CAN BE AN ACT OF LOVE."
—FRANK SONNENBERG

"YOUR JOB ISN'T TO GIVE YOUR KIDS EVERYTHING. IT'S TO ENCOURAGE THEM AND HELP THEM FIND WHAT THEY NEED."

—JIM MARGRAFF

"THE GREATEST JOY A PARENT CAN HAVE AND AN AFFIRMATION OF BEING AN OUTSTANDING ROLE MODEL IS WHEN YOUR CHILD TELLS YOU SHE WANTS TO BE JUST LIKE YOU. SO BE THE MOST OUTSTANDING YOU BECAUSE WHEN YOU BECOME A PARENT ONE DAY, YOUR CHILDREN WILL BE PROUD TO BE JUST LIKE YOU."

—KAILIN GOW

"IT'S AMAZING WHAT
YOU'LL DO FOR YOUR
CHILD, ISN'T IT?"

—DIANE CHAMBERLAIN

"CLEANING YOUR HOUSE WHILE YOUR KIDS ARE STILL GROWING UP IS LIKE SHOVELING THE SIDEWALK BEFORE IT STOPS SNOWING."

—PHYLLIS DILLER

"WHAT IS A HOME WITHOUT CHILDREN? QUIET."
—HENNY YOUNGMAN

"MY CHILDREN ARE THE REASON I LAUGH, SMILE,
AND WANT TO GET UP EVERY MORNING."
—GENA LEE NOLIN

"MOST CHILDREN THREATEN AT TIMES TO RUN AWAY FROM HOME.
THIS IS THE ONLY THING THAT KEEPS SOME PARENTS GOING."

—PHYLLIS DILLER

"FEW THINGS ARE MORE SATISFYING THAN SEEING YOUR CHILDREN HAVE TEENAGERS OF THEIR OWN."

—DOUG LARSON

"WHAT IT'S LIKE TO BE A PARENT: IT'S ONE OF THE HARDEST THINGS YOU'LL EVER DO BUT IN EXCHANGE IT TEACHES YOU THE MEANING OF UNCONDITIONAL LOVE."

—NICHOLAS SPARKS

"IT'S NOT ONLY CHILDREN WHO GROW.
PARENTS DO TOO. AS MUCH AS WE
WATCH TO SEE WHAT OUR CHILDREN
DO WITH THEIR LIVES, THEY ARE
WATCHING US TO SEE WHAT WE DO
WITH OURS. I CAN'T TELL MY CHILDREN
TO REACH FOR THE SUN. ALL I CAN DO
IS REACH FOR IT, MYSELF."

—JOYCE MAYNARD

"GOOD PARENTS HARDLY PARENT. THEY
LET THEIR KIDS LEARN, FAIL, AND GROW
WITHOUT INTERFERENCE."
—TREVOR CARSS

"YOU CAN'T RAISE KIDS TO BELIEVE LIFE IS ALWAYS GOING TO BE SMOOTH. SOMETIMES LIFE THROWS ROCKS AT YOU, AND WHEN THAT HAPPENS, THEY NEED TO LEARN TO DODGE WHEN THEY CAN AND GET BACK UP IF THEY'RE HIT. YOU NEED TO TEACH THEM TO HANDLE THE ROCKS."

—SARAH MORGAN

"ALL OF US HAVE MOMENTS
IN OUR LIVES THAT TEST OUR
COURAGE. TAKING CHILDREN
INTO A HOUSE WITH WHITE
CARPET IS ONE OF THEM."
—ERMA BOMBECK

"YOUR KIDS REQUIRE YOU MOST OF ALL TO LOVE THEM FOR WHO THEY ARE, NOT TO SPEND YOUR WHOLE TIME TRYING TO CORRECT THEM."

—BILL AYERS

"ONE FACT THAT I DISCOVERED AS A PARENT IS THAT WE MUST TREASURE OUR CHILD EVERY DAY OF THEIR LIFE. A CHILD DOES NOT REMAIN THE SAME; THEY ARE A DIFFERENT PERSON AT VARIOUS STAGES IN THEIR LIVES."

—KILROY J. OLDSTER

"NO ONE IS PERFECT AND PARENTING IS
EXCELLENT AT MAGNIFYING THAT FACT."

—J. S. B. MORSE

"PARENTS ARE NEVER SURE THAT THEY HAVE DONE THE RIGHT THING. THEY CAN ONLY DO WHAT THEY THINK IS RIGHT."

—JAMES HERRIOT

"ONE THING I HAD LEARNED FROM WATCHING CHIMPANZEES WITH THEIR INFANTS IS THAT HAVING A CHILD SHOULD BE FUN."
—JANE GOODALL

# THE DOGS

**PUG**
Nena: 3 years
Jack: 13 weeks

**AMERICAN ESKIMO**
Atka: 10 years
Kayu: 5 months

**CHIHUAHUA**
Twee: 4 years
Max: 13 weeks

**FRENCH BULLDOG**
Walter: 2 years
Vence: 10 weeks

**BASSET HOUND**
Cyan Pepper: 12 weeks
Jalapeno Popper: 12 weeks

**ENGLISH BULLDOG**
Emily Rose: 4 years
Tycoon: 14 weeks

**CARDIGAN WELSH CORGI**
Edison: 9 weeks
Dallas: 9 weeks

**DALMATIAN**
Elizabeth: 8 weeks
Cece: 8 weeks

**ENGLISH SPRINGER
SPANIEL**
Bella: 4 years
Nessie: 7 weeks

**CAVALIER KING
CHARLES SPANIEL**
Romeo: 3 years
Pete: 12 weeks

**SHORT HAIRED
DACHSHUND**
Huckleberry: 2 years
Olive: 8 weeks

**PORTUGUESE WATER DOG**
Sky: 10 weeks
Gregg: 10 weeks

**POMERANIAN**
Melody: 4 years
Buddy: 4 months

**JACK RUSSELL TERRIER**
Ivy: 18 months
London: 12 weeks

**NORWICH TERRIER**
Wren: 2½ years
Cleo: 9 weeks

**SIBERIAN HUSKY**
Stella: 18 months
Gidget: 8 weeks

**LONG HAIRED DACHSHUND**
Hazelnut: 2 years
Blackberry: 8 weeks

**GREAT PYRENEES**
Carly: 11 weeks
Smokey: 11 weeks

**GERMAN SHEPHERD**
Petey: 2 years, 8 months
Huey: 4 months

**AUSTRALIAN SHEPHERD**
Hazel: 1 year
Riley: 10 months

**BOSTON TERRIER**
Tabatha: 4 years
Bowie: 14 weeks

**GOLDEN RETRIEVER**
Cash: 3 years
Buttercup: 8 weeks

**MINIATURE PINSCHER**
Mr. Bojangles: 9 years
Tiny Dancer: 6 months

**FRENCH BULLDOG**
Ula: 3 years
Ollie: 15 weeks

**RHODESIAN RIDGEBACK**
Hazelnut: 3 years
Leo: 8 weeks

**BEAGLE**
Gerald: 2 years
Paden: 7 weeks

**MINIATURE BEAGLE**
Pearl: 3 years
Tiny: 8 months

**GERMAN SHORTHAIRED
POINTER**
Ceilidh: 7 years
Rae: 7 weeks

**LABRADOR RETRIEVER**
Shlep: 4 years
Hintele: 4 months

**CHOCOLATE LABRADOR
RETRIEVER**
Seadoo: 11 weeks
Kawasaki: 11 weeks

# THANK YOU

Photographing one dog by itself can be a test in patience. Photographing two dogs together is a whole other feat. There are many people who helped make this book a reality.

The biggest thank you to my husband Ryan and daughters Neve and Laine, who are my everything.

To my dad and mom, Leslie and Susie, for their unwavering love and support, which allows me to always follow my ambitions.

Thank you to Leah Zarra at Skyhorse Publishing for seeing a new perspective for this book.

Thank you to Lori Cannava, an incredible friend and retoucher.

All of the images in this book were captured at Go Studios. Thank you Halley for always providing a safe, friendly, and professional place to photograph animals.

Thanks to Linda Hanrahan for her tireless work in bringing together these incredible dog pairs.

Thank you to all the wonderful dog owners and handlers who were part of this project. Thy Cavagnaro, Annie Wasserman, Susan Gural, Rita Wagoner, Stephanie Teed, Simon Goldin, Carolyn McGarry, Patty Mitchell, Jill Kiernan, Sue Lucatorto, Kimberlee Young, Tracey Monahan, Donald Snyder, Patricia Sulzberger, Jamie Oliva, Sheryl Schulze, Andrew Kalmanash, Irene and Drew Rabinowitz, Cathy Iacopelli, Barbara and Doug Kahl, Lisa M. Hoffman, Sharon and Henry Scully, Sue Sobel, Jane O'Halloran, Ada Nieves, Linda Anthony, Jerrie Champlin, Bob Baranowski, Jean Buscaglia- Yurkiewicz, Betty McDonnell, and Rick Busda.

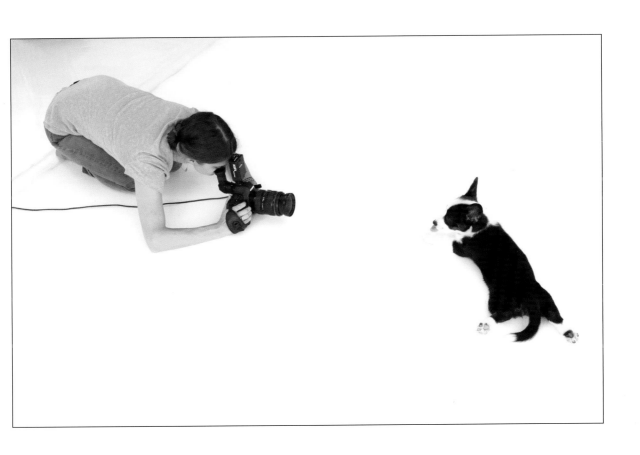